We all have big dreams.

Sometimes it takes
hard work to make
them come true.

Sometimes all we have
to do is imagine. . . .

DREAM TRUE!

In your dreams, anything is possible.
Take a deep breath and together,
let's imagine a world where
we can be anything.

Dream Board

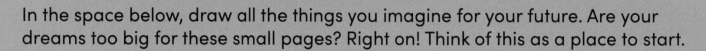

In the space below, draw all the things you imagine for your future. Are your dreams too big for these small pages? Right on! Think of this as a place to start.

Dream with Love

One way to imagine your future self is to think of the things you care about right now. How many of the acitvities below do you love? What would you add to this list? Write your favs in the blank spaces below!

Caring for a Pet

♡ Love it!   ♡ Like it.

♡ I'd rather not.

Cooking

♡ Love it!   ♡ Like it.

♡ I'd rather not.

Gaming

♡ Love it!   ♡ Like it.

♡ I'd rather not.

Growing a Plant

♡ Love it!   ♡ Like it.

♡ I'd rather not.

Competing in a Sport

♡ Love it!   ♡ Like it.

♡ I'd rather not.

Playing an Instrument

♡ Love it!   ♡ Like it.

♡ I'd rather not.

Filming a Video or Movie

♡ Love it!   ♡ Like it.

♡ I'd rather not.

Reading a Book

♡ Love it!   ♡ Like it.

♡ I'd rather not.

Where Is Your Heart?

When you think about your future self, where do you imagine living? Draw a heart on each line below to mark the choice you prefer. The closer your heart is to a choice, the more you prefer it. If you like both choices equally, draw your heart in the middle of the line.

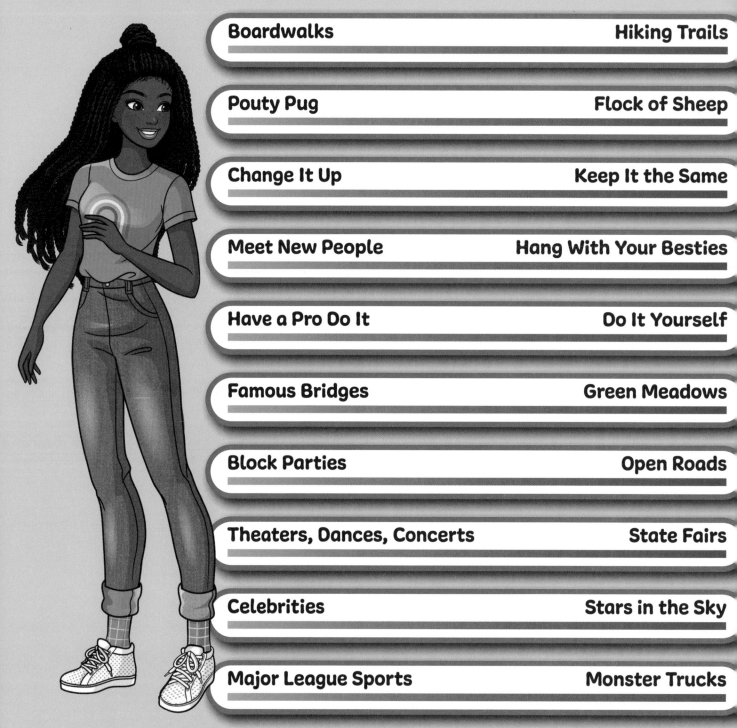

Boardwalks	Hiking Trails
Pouty Pug	Flock of Sheep
Change It Up	Keep It the Same
Meet New People	Hang With Your Besties
Have a Pro Do It	Do It Yourself
Famous Bridges	Green Meadows
Block Parties	Open Roads
Theaters, Dances, Concerts	State Fairs
Celebrities	Stars in the Sky
Major League Sports	Monster Trucks

Key: Are your hearts mostly in the orange areas? You might have big city dreams. If your hearts are mostly in the purple areas, a country life might make you happy. Are your hearts mostly in the middle? Your dreamhouse might be in a town.

No matter where your heart is today, your future could take you anywhere. Unscramble the letters to find people and places to love wherever you go.

Follow your samder _____

and keep your heart nope _____!

Happy Thoughts

Color in the words below. Notice how each word makes you feel.

nature

color

flavors

discovery

health

environment

sports

animals

family

friendship

stories

galaxy

rcle the words that gave you a boost of joy, then find them in this word search grid.

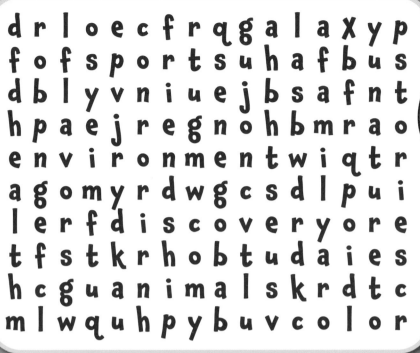

```
d r l o e c f r q g a l a x y p
f o f s p o r t s u h a f b u s
d b l y v n i u e j b s a f n t
h p a e j r e g n o h b m r a o
e n v i r o n m e n t w i q t r
a g o m y r d w g c s d l p u i
l e r f d i s c o v e r y o r e
t f s t k r h o b t u d a i e s
h c g u a n i m a l s k r d t c
m l w q u h p y b u v c o l o r
```

Draw ways you can spend more time with these joyful things.

Oh Where, Oh Where Would You Go?

The world is BIG! Where in the world would you like to visit? Fill in the postcards below with names and descriptions of places you want to visit one day!

Greetings from _____ !

_____ isn't the same without you!

It's beautiful here in _____ !

Hello from _____!

Missing you from _____!

The weather's great in _____!

What Are You Passionate About?

Malibu and Brooklyn want to protect the planet. Do you dream of protecting the planet too? Here's the game plan! How many of these things can you do? Check them off!

Comin' at you live from...

...a cleaner planet!

- [ ] **Unplug your devices when fully charged.**
- [ ] **Turn off running water.**
- [ ] **Compost! (Worms love it!)**
- [ ] **Start a garden.**
- [ ] **Drink from reusable water bottles.**
- [ ] **Move greener: carpool, walk, or ride bikes.**
- [ ] **Pick up trash near rivers, lakes, and oceans.**

What are you passionate about protecting? Make a list below.

Hello, You

Draw a picture of you at your happiest. Who is with you? Where are you? What are you doing?

Now draw your future self. Who is with you? Where are you? What are you doing?

DREAM BOLD!

The beauty of dreams is that there are no limits. *You* have no limits. What will you do with your limitless potential?

Dream of Change

Sometimes things get in the way of our dreams. Some of those things are small, like missing the bus on the way to a friend's house. Some of those things are big, like not having enough money to ride the bus. Sometimes dreams require change. Can you think of big things that might stand in the way of someone's dreams? Make a list here.

ick one of the things from your list. Make a poster explaining why this thing
nust change. Can you imagine a world where this thing doesn't exist?

DREAM IT,
DO IT.

Because You Are Strong . . . Imagine Becoming a Firefighter!

Imagine you hear an alarm. You jump out of bed, slide down a fire pole, and pull on your gear. With a hop, you join your team in the fire truck. Maybe you climb the ladder, use the fire hose, or carry someone to safety! You are a firefighter. How does it feel?

Before joining a fire department, people attend a special school and pass a firefighting test. Unscramble the letters to find out how the firefighting academy would train you.

1. Lift weights and run drills to idulb _____ strong muscles.

2. Jump rope to make sure your thera _____ and snugl _____ are healthy.

3. cicerapt _____ driving the truck, climbing the ladder, and using the hose.

If I trained like a firefighter, I would have big, strong muscles!

Think about how you have grown bigger and stronger.

I used to need help to _____ .

Now, all on my own, I am strong enough to _____ .

Someday I want to be strong enough to _____ !

Because You Are Brave . . . Imagine Becoming an Astronaut!

When astronauts go to space, they know they are risking their lives. Even experienced astronauts feel scared during a launch. But they want to explore and discover. It's their dream, and they must be brave to follow their dream.

Fear can get in the way of our dreams. If Brooklyn dreamed of becoming an astronaut instead of joining a professional ballet company, she would have to get through many fears to follow her dream.

Complete the maze by finding your way to every gold-star achievement. Cross out any stop signs that get in your way.

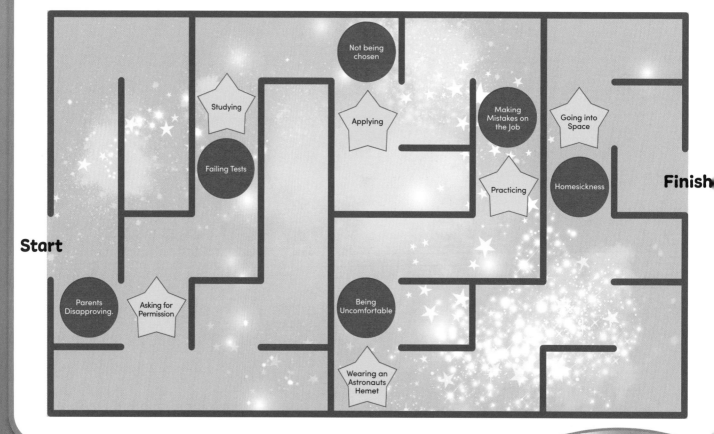

Start

Finish

Not being chosen

Studying

Applying

Making Mistakes on the Job

Going into Space

Failing Tests

Practicing

Homesickness

Parents Disapproving.

Asking for Permission

Being Uncomfortable

Wearing an Astronauts Hemet

Think of a time you were brave. Fill out this badge of courage to celebrate your act of bravery!

braved a fear of

in order to

24

Because You Are Creative . . . Imagine Becoming a Fashion Designer!

Imagine you are fitting a dress you made for the red carpet, but your client isn't happy. The belt is uncomfortable. The fabric is the wrong color. And she wants it to be more flowery. You only have a few days to make these final alterations.

You imagine one million changes that would make the client happy. You pick three changes you can do by the deadline.

1. Replace the belt with a sash.
2. Dye the fabric.
3. Add rose embroidery

You sketch the dress with the changes to show your client:

Your client swoons! You've designed a winner. Problem solved!

Because You Are Observant...
Imagine Becoming a Doctor!

Being observant means you are quick to notice changes. Doctors need to notice changes in their patients to find out what is making them sick. Then, they can choose the right treatment to make them feel better.

Think of a time you were the first to notice a change—or imagine you were the first. How did it make you feel? Circle as many as you want.

Smart   **Helpful**   **Powerful**

Kind   **Important**   **Compassionate**

Pretend you are a doctor. In the situations below, what medical device would you use to help your patient? Draw a line to match the device and the situation.

You want to:

1. **Check someone's heart**
2. **Protect a wound**
3. **Take someone's temperature**
4. **Give someone a shot**

You need a:

a. **Bandage**
b. **Thermometer**
c. **Stethoscope**
d. **Syringe**

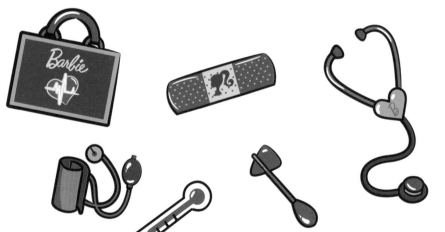

Answers: 1. c, 2. a, 3. b, 4. d

Because You Feel It . . . Imagine Becoming a Musician!

Write the name of your favorite song.

_____

_____

_____

_____

Music is made up of sounds that make us feel. Think about your favorite song. How does it make you feel? Check off as many emotions as you like.

- ☐ Joyful
- ☐ Sad
- ☐ Proud
- ☐ Pumped Up
- ☐ Inspired
- ☐ Dreamy

I feel pumped up and inspired when I sing "Can't Stop Us."

What do you like best about your favorite song?

- ☐ **Melody** (The pattern of notes we sing.)
- ☐ **Beat** (The steady pulse we feel. We can dance to a beat.)
- ☐ **Rhythm** (A pattern of sounds on a beat. We can clap a rhythm.)
- ☐ **Chords and Harmonies** (The groups of notes we hear at once.)
- ☐ **Lyrics** (The words in a song. They often have patterns, like rhymes.)

Because You Are Innovative . . . Imagine Becoming a Chef!

Being innovative means coming up with new ideas. Imagine you are a chef. You travel all over the world tasting foods and ingredients. The flavors you taste ignite your imagination. At your restaurant, you create innovative dishes. Fill in the story about your award-winning creation!

The winner of the Gold Star Chef Award is . . . you!

I stepped off the plane. It was my first time in _____.
(place name)

I went straight to the annual food festival. It was huge! The air smelled

like _____. I saw foods I've tried before, like
(yummy smell)

_____. I ordered my favorite. The vendor also made
(foods you love)

juice from local ingredients. "I'll try one," I said. She handed me a bright

_____ juice. It smelled like_____.
(color)   (flavor)

I took a sip. It was _____! It gave me the idea for
(word to describe food)

a new dish. I added a_____. I served it on
(fruit or vegetable)

_____ dishes. I called it_____!
(color)   (name of dish)

I love coming up with new recipes. When I get an idea for a new dish,

I feel _____.
(emotion)

Because You Have a Story to Tell . . . Imagine Becoming a Filmmaker!

People who create films start with a storyboard. Make your own by drawing the parts of a film!

1. Introduction

2. Problem

3. Solution

4. Closing

Each shot of a storyboard captures key elements: subject, background, camera shot, and the camera's movement. Try to get those into your pictures!

Because You Ask Questions . . . Imagine Becoming a Scientist!

You've been working in your lab all day, and you might be on the verge of a major discovery! You focus and experiment. At first, you don't believe what you see. You repeat the experiment to confirm the results. "This needs further study!" you say. You are a scientist. How do you feel?

Scientists are curious about the universe. They wonder how things work. Then they gather information, do experiments, make guesses, test their guesses, and share what they discover. What questions do you have about the following topics?

Fossils and Dinosaurs: _____

Outer Space: _____

Plants: _____

Animals: _____

Weather: _____

Earth's Surface: _____

Soil and Growing Food: _____

Diseases and Health: _____

Great questions! Pick the question you care about most. Draw a star next to it.

Where can you look for the answer to your question? Circle as many as you'd like to try.

Ask a teacher or librarian.

Go to a museum, planetarium, or park.

Read a book.

Watch a documentary.

Look in an encyclopedia.

Write to an expert.

Now try to find the answer! Be sure to ask an adult for help and permission. Remember, scientist, all information is good information. It can get you closer to finding answers. It might inspire you to ask new questions. Write what you learn here.

_____

_____

_____

_____

Because You Are Compassionate . . . Imagine Becoming a Vet!

Veterinarians care deeply about the animals they treat. If you saw a dog limping, what would you do? How often do pets need a checkup? A vet would know because they want to make sure animals are feeling their 100% best!

Can you tell which animal is sick? Read the facts. Then circle the pet with a fever.

Healthy Temperatures:
cats and dogs: **101 to 102.5°F**
birds: **102 to 109°F**

turtles: **77 to 81°F**
rabbits: **102 to 103°F**

horses: **99 to 101°F**
fish: **75 to 80°F**

80°F   **104°F**   **107°F**

101°F   **80°F**   **102°F**   **99°F**

Healing sick animals is only one way of caring. What does caring look like for you?

Future vets graduate high school, college, and then veterinary college. They go to school for twenty years!

VISITOR Barbie

33

Answer: cat

Because You Are Motivated . . . Imagine Becoming a Dancer!

After years of training, you finally got the part. You practiced the steps for months. You listened to the music until it became part of you. Your job tonight is to dance your heart out and entertain your audience. How do you feel?

rofessional dancers have to bring the energy every day. When rehearsal starts, whether dancers are tired, or bored, or cranky, they must be ready to give it their all.

ry these motivational tips in your own life.
ill in the stars to rate how much they helped.

Find gratitude!

Sometimes we try our best and still don't reach our goals. Be thankful for the goals you've already reached. Celebrating your abilities welcomes new ones.

Explore!

When we are focused on a goal 100%, we can get bogged down. Do something out of the ordinary. A new experience can give you fresh ideas and you'll be excited to get back to work.

Connect!

Relax with friends, family, a pet, or just yourself! Being with people you love will spark joy.

Stay in the moment!

When we practice, practice, practice, our minds can wander. We can lose excitement about an activity we love. Find a way to make each day special—set a small goal, change up a routine, test out a new idea. Excitement is motivation!

Because You Have Goals . . . Imagine Becoming an Athlete!

Sometimes goals are all about winning games and scoring points.

Match the sport to the goal.

You can also set a goal to try something new, enjoy the moment, support teammates, or beat your personal best. Goals help us try a little bit harder. They give us moments to celebrate.

If you put in a little extra effort, what goal could you reach?

_____

When you reach your goal, write how it makes you feel:

_____

Are you struggling to achieve your goal? Cross it out and write a new one. Be proud that you keep reaching!

Answers: 1. d, 2. c, 3. b, 4. a

Because You Care . . .
Imagine Becoming an Activist!

Activists take action to make political and social change. What would you like to change in the world?

_____

_____

_____

_____

_____

_____

You can make a difference!

Here are some ways to get active for the change you want to see. Make sure to get help and permission from an adult. Circle as many as you'd like to try.

1. **Join peaceful marches and protests.**

2. **Raise money for organizations through bake sales or craft sales.**

3. **Volunteer for causes and non-profits you care about.**

4. **Start or join a club at school. Run for student government.**

5. **Write letters to your elected government officials.**

6. **Educate your friends, family, and people in your neighborhood.**

Because You Are a Leader . . . Imagine Becoming a CEO!

You step off the elevator and walk to your office. On the way, you say, "Good morning," to your staff. You have time to make one phone call. You dial the phone. "Congratulations!" you say. "Your project is approved! I'll tell the team this morning." You dash off to the staff meeting. "I'm excited to tell you about our next big project," you say. "You are going to *love* it!"

EO stands for chief executive officer. They lead companies big and small. The best CEOs inspire the people who work for them.

What do you think it means to be inspirational? _____

_____

_____

Who inspires you? _____

_____

_____

CEOs also make tough choices. Imagine you are a CEO. What choices would you make? For each question, circle as many answers as you'd like.

My company would make . . .

a. healthy foods.

b. fun games.

c. safe pet toys.

d. creative clothing.

I would hire . . .

a. people excited to learn.

b. people from different backgrounds.

c. people who need a second chance.

d. people with the most experience.

My company would be famous for . . .

a. making the coolest products.

b. being environmentally friendly.

c. earning lots of money.

d. improving peoples' lives.

I would give my employees . . .

a. kindness and respect.

b. chances to learn and improve.

c. whatever they wanted.

d. the ability to work from home.

Do you feel inspired to start this company?

Yes, here's my business card!

No, I would feel more inspired if . . .

Name: _____

Title: _____ **CEO** _____

Company name: _____

_____

_____

_____

Because You Are Resilient . . . Imagine Becoming a Farmer!

Farmers grow the food we eat. It's an important job and a big one! Farmers spend most of their day outside. From dawn until dusk, they take care of their crops, animals, machines, and land.

Since farmers rely on natural elements like rain, sun, and soil, they need to be resilient. That means they know what to do when things go wrong. Can you think of a time when you've been resilient? Write or draw about it here.

ver hear of cooperative farming? It's a way of sharing land, work, and earnings with group of other farmers and people in the community. That way, no one person has bear all the responsibility of running the farm, and lots of people benefit.

If you were to start a cooperative farm, who would you want on your team?

_____

_____

Because You Are Confident . . . Imagine Becoming an Equestrian!

You slip the bridle over the mare's ears. "Good girl," you say warmly. The mare snorts, happy to work with you. You check that the riding gear is safe and secure. Then you step into the stirrup and mount the horse. You are ready to ride! How do you feel?

orses are smart, powerful creatures. But horses are easily frightened. If the horse
frightened, it will act without thinking and might get hurt. A rider can keep
horse safe by feeling calm and confident.

Horses understand how people are feeling!

When a rider feels sure of herself, the horse trusts the rider. It can follow commands instead of acting out of fear.

One way to feel confident is to prepare. Trace this maze until you are confident you know the way. Then complete the maze with a pencil or pen.

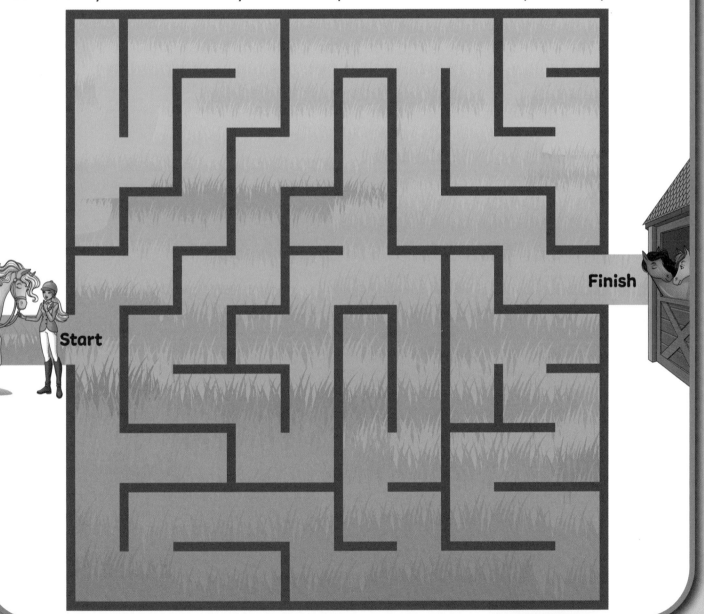

Start

Finish

Because You Are Logical . . . Imagine Becoming a Video Game Programmer!

Video game programmers work with game designers, artists, and testers. The programmer turns their ideas into code, the language of computers. Use your imagination and follow the steps to create a game.

1. **Enter your name to start your game.**

   Adventures of Super _____

2. **Work out the basic game play with the game designer.**

   My character's powers are: _____

   My character's level-one challenge is: _____

3. **Describe how the game should look to a game artist.**

   Circle as many choices as you like.

   Characters Are:
   - **Mermaids**
   - **Aliens**
   - **Ghouls**
   - **Astronauts**

   Mood Is:
   - **Epic**
   - **Scary**
   - **Chill**
   - **Funny**

   Style Looks:
   - **Realistic**
   - **Spacey**
   - **Magical**
   - **Retro**

4. **The game designer plays a prototype of the game. She will change the prototype to make sure the game is fun to play.**

   Add to the game by filling in as many extras as you like.

   Happy catchphrase:_____

   Sidekick's name _____

   Helpful gadget: _____

   Bonus points for: _____

   Bonus points earn: _____

5. **You code a build of the game, test it, fix any bugs you find, and repeat until the game comes to life. Draw your gameplay here:**

You're ready to ship your game.

Congratulations, you brought an idea to life!

Because You Are Energetic . . .
Imagine Becoming a Teacher!

To be a good teacher, you have to be comfortable speaking in front of an audience, sharing knowledge and ideas, listening to others, and adapting to challenges. That's a lot of work!

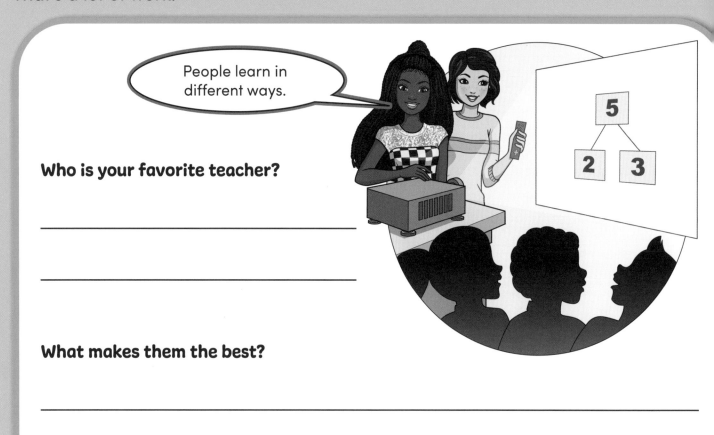

People learn in different ways.

Who is your favorite teacher?

_____

_____

What makes them the best?

_____

_____

Pilots do more than fly. They are responsible for the safety of the plane, passengers, and even people on the ground! They have a big job.

These are just some of the things a pilot has to do:

- **Conduct a safety check**
- **Review the flight plan**
- **Read the plane's gauges**

- **Use the plane's controls to fly**
- **Practice staying calm and focused**
- **Understand the math and physics of flight**

A major part of being a good pilot, and a good teammate, is clear communication. When pilots talk to Air Traffic Control over the radio, they follow specific rules to avoid any confusion.

To start a radio communication, follow these steps:

1. **Say the name of the person or place you're calling.**

2. **Identify your aircraft. If the name of the aircraft has a letter at the end, pilots use a code word that starts with that letter instead of the letter itself. So, for a Baron 536B aircraft, you'd say, "Baron Five Three Six Bravo."**

3. **Ask a question or share information.**

4. **Say the word "over."**

You try! Pretend you are piloting a Barbie 222B aircraft. You want to request clearance for landing at New York Flight Service Station.

Over the radio, you'd say: _____

_____

Just think, you could be piloting the plane that brings Malibu to visit me in NYC!

Answer: New York Flight Service Station, Barbie Two Two Bravo, request clearance for landing, over.

47

DREAM BIG!

What you do with your life matters. People change the world. Choices change the world. How do you want to change the world?

Ask Big Questions

Meet four women who followed their dreams. What would you ask them? Match each question to as many women as you want!

How did you choose this career?

How many years did you go to school?

What is your favorite part of your job?

How have you changed the world?

How do you want the world to change?

I am ready to ask questions. I keep a list of what I want to know!

Shonda Rhimes: She is Black and American. She wrote scripts for TV shows. Now she owns her own company, Shondaland. She makes TV shows, movies, podcasts, and more!

Amy O'Sullivan: She is white and American. She is an emergency room nurse in New York City. At the same time, she has three daughters with her partner, Tiffany. She became a hero saving lives in the Covid-19 pandemic.

Misty Copeland: She is Black and American. She started ballet lessons when she was thirteen years old. Most ballet dancers begin training at three years old. She was the first African American female principal dancer at a major ballet company.

Sky Brown: She is British-Japanese. She was born in Japan. When she was ten years old, she became the youngest professional skateboarder. She was the youngest Olympian to win a medal for Great Britain.

What if you could meet anyone in the world?

Who would you meet? _____

What would you ask? _____

What would you want to be asked? _____

What would your answer be? _____

Every person is important. Who is important to you?
Draw yourself with that person.

Barbie

An important person to me is _____.

One big thing they've done is _____.

My biggest question for them is _____.

Do Good Work

The kinds of jobs we do can make a big difference. We can use our jobs to help people, express ourselves, or celebrate something important. If you had these jobs, what would be your biggest goal?

Teacher: _____

Doctor: _____

Game Developer: _____

Veterinarian: _____

Chef: _____

Fashion Designer: _____

eople create new jobs. You can create your own job too!
ircle as many jobs as you want from the list below.

activist	dancer	filmmaker	teacher
athlete	doctor	firefighter	vet
astronaut	equestrian	musician	video game programmer
CEO	farmer	pilot	
chef	fashion designer	scientist	

Hmm, should I become the first singer-dancer-musician-astronaut?

Now put those jobs together. You've made a new job!

What would your job be called? _____

_____

What would your job be like?

Shape the Future

Which of these do you hope your future holds? Check off as many as you want!

New styles of music

New rules at school

New laws

New job

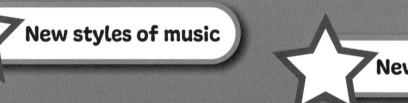

I want to sing on stages all around the world.

I create new dance routines all the time!

New dances

New hairstyles

New holidays

New places to visit

New social media apps

New clothing styles

Choose one of your new ideas. Draw it here!

Make Big Waves

Some people use "simple" things to make big waves in the world—one word, thread, or step at a time. Finish each sentence using the words below.

WORD BANK

motto	balance	camera
words	makeup	mindfulness
thread and fabric	voices	passion

1. Beauticians use _____ to transform people's faces. They use precision, creativity, and out-of-the-box vision to make every look unique!

2. Fashion designers sew using_____ to make culture-shifting outfits.

3. Athletes need to use_____ to skateboard and surf. Dancers also use that to stay on beat.

4. Podcasters and radio show hosts use their_____ to talk on air. They can speak about important topics, making the world better and more equal.

5. Photographers use a _____ to make art. They take photos and make films.

6. Tennis players feel _____ when they play a sport that they truly love.

7. Authors use _____ to write and tell stories.

8. Famous inspirational speakers often repeat the same _____ to uplift listeners and improve the world.

9. Health and wellness instructors use the calming practice of _____ to help young people thrive.

Answers: 1. makeup, 2. thread and fabric, 3. balance, 4. voices, 5. camera, 6. passion, 7. words, 8. motto, 9. mindfulness

57

DREAM STRONG!

To make your dreams come true, you must take care of YOU. This means tapping into your feelings, listening to your body, being kind to yourself, and resting.

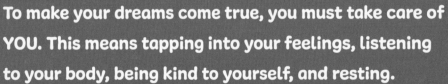

Stay Calm and Carry On

Draw a picture of your most calm, rested self.
Remember what this looks and feels like!

I Feel...

Being aware of our feelings will help us make good decisions, ask good questions, and know when we've had enough. Write about when you feel...

Tired: _____

Inspired: _____

Confused: _____

Disappointed: _____

Excited: _____

Happy: _____

Sad: _____

Proud: _____

Mad: _____

Nervous: _____

Give it Time

You are going to feel all the feelings. What activities will help you during different emotional times? Fill in as many activties as you want from the list on the right. Add your own ideas too!

Tired Time: _____

Inspired Time: _____

Confused Time: _____

Disappointed Time: _____

Excited Time: _____

Happy Time: _____

Sad Time: _____

Proud Time: _____

Mad Time: _____

Nervous Time: _____

Remember, feelings come and go!

Write about or draw it	**Run, dance, move**
Take a break	**Take breaths**
Ask questions	**Give big hugs**
Look on the bright side	**Think of a friendly face**
Enjoy it	**Play a silly game**
Tell a friend	**Get a good night's sleep**
Cry it out	

And I am always here to listen!

Rest and Recharge

Dreamers need their strength. Which activities make you feel your best? Color the pictures and circle your favorite.

Watching a movie or reading a book.

Moving your body.

Spending time with family and friends.

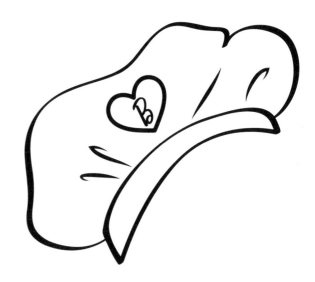

Making a treat.

Secret Passwords

Do you ever feel anxious when you're about to do something big? Try telling yourself these things.

I am **loved**.

I can ask for **help**.

I would be my **friend**.

I can take a **break**.

Bad feelings **come** and **go**.

I can **try**.

Find the bold words in the word search below.

g d h n u i m s w g o X
b r e a k d f l h u j t
s h l b u s c o m e c h
t b p h u q r v t g e t
f w t b e h a e h b u r
q k f r i e n d t i h y

Dear Me

Sometimes our feelings are so big it helps to write them out in a journal. Use the space below to help you get started.

Dear journal,

Today was_____. I was able to

_____, just like I always dreamed I would.

It took a lot of_____and_____,

but it happened.

Tomorrow I will_____. I love that

I_____._____makes me special

and makes me_____.

Sincerely,

Wonderful Me

Motivational Mantras

Keep on saying good things to yourself! They not only make you feel better and stronger, but they are also 100% true. (Ask Malibu, she lives by it!) Repeat each sentence in the morning, or whenever you need a confidence booster.

I believe in myself.

I make good choices and mistakes. Both are okay.

I can be anything.

I am allowed to take up space.

I have a voice that should be heard.

I am a leader.

I know how to follow and be supportive.

I can try again if I make a mistake.

I can make a difference in small and big ways.

I am strong.

I am vulnerable.

I make change.

I matter.

I try new things.

I am an awesome person.

I love myself.

I am different.

I am at peace.

I am loved.

I am loving.

I am proud of myself.

I like to learn and better myself.

I am a good friend.

Barbie

DREAM TOGETHER!

When you go after your dreams, it helps to have people in your corner. People rooting for you, people you can learn from. When you have a community to support you, you can dream even bigger.

No One Works Alone

People in different careers can inspire us and help us reach our dreams. We can partner or "network" so that our work helps us all.

Can you pick the right partner for these professionals?

1. **Who can help a filmmaker create a screenplay?**

2. **Who can help an astronaut prepare to go to space?**

3. **Who can help a video game programmer with tech questions?**

4. **Who can help a model with her wardrobe?**

5. **Who can help a real estate agent repair a house for sale?**

6. **Who can help a pilot get ready for a flight?**

7. **Who can help a doctor take care of patients?**

WORD BANK

a. **a writer**

b. **a fashion designer**

c. **a scientist**

d. **a nurse**

e. **a flight attendant**

f. **a software engineer**

g. **a construction worker**

Answers: 1. a, 2. c, 3. f, 4. b, 5. g, 6. e, 7. d

Better Together

In the activity below, we see that while one thing can be powerful, more than one can be extraordinary. Match the single things below to the larger group.

1. A person can raise their voice.

2. A drop of water makes a tiny splash.

3. A brick is a building block.

4. A page introduces an idea.

5. A flower is beautiful.

a. A book tells the whole story.

b. A garden feeds butterflies and bees.

c. An ocean can cut through stone.

d. Thousands of bricks make a building.

e. A community can make a change.

My little sister loves soccer. She can't play alone. She needs to be part of something bigger—**a team!**

Answers: 1. e, 2. c, 3. d, 4. a, 5. b

Give a Power Boost

Being part of a community means encouraging your friends as they chase their dreams too! What are some encouraging words or phrases you can say to your besties? Fill in the blanks below!

1. You created something s__eci__l.

2. You made a lot of prog__ess!

3. T__us__ yourself; you've got this.

4. I am here to lis__en if you need me.

5. It is okay to take a __rea__. Let's go for a walk.

Answers: 1. special, 2. progress, 3. Trust, 4. listen, 5. break.

s much as words can encourage, they can also do harm.
ere are some activities to help you think about the words
e use and how we use them.

Imagine you and your friends want to help the environment. Your parents take you to City Hall to organize a cleanup of the park. The clerk at the office is surprised. "They're just kids. Can they do it?" the clerk says. You start to wonder if you're really up to the task.

What could your parents say to get rid of the doubt? Underline the most empowering sentence.

Even though they're kids, we think they can do it.

Yeah, they're kids! Kids can do anything.

"Just" minimizes—makes smaller. It makes it sound like something isn't a big deal or isn't enough. Like, we're not *just* cleaning up a park. We're cleaning up a park! That is something—don't say it like it's nothing.

Imagine a girl in your class said she wants to be president. But a bully said she could never do that because she's "just a girl." The girl is hurt and starts to doubt her dream.

What could you say to give her confidence? Underline the most empowering sentence.

Girls can be presidents too.

Girls are presidents.

"Too" can be othering. It sounds like someone else is supposed to be president. Girls are presidents. Why is that so hard for people to say?

Better Things to Say

When we don't feel good about ourselves, it's tough to reach for our dreams. There are 600,000 words in the English language. Let's pick the ones that make us feel better, not worse.

> So, I'm a lively person. When I get excited, it shows! I feel upset when people say I have "big energy." It sounds like a problem. Like I'm "too much."

> Yeah, like you're supposed to be quiet or not draw attention. I think girls get that a lot.

Daisy is lively, exuberant, and engaged. Can you think of other positive words?

_____

> I get teased for being "all emo" or "mopey," but I'm just listening to, thinking about, and feeling the world around me.

> Because you're quiet, people sometimes think you don't care. But you care so much! And it shows in your music.

Skipper is deeply feeling, private, and internal. Can you think of other positive words?

_____

Have your words ever hurt someone? What were they?	What could you have said instead?	Would you like to apologize for your words? Practice your apology here.
_____	_____	_____
_____	_____	_____

Here's the thing: There are billions of people on this planet. That means there are billions of different ways to be.

So just be you, no matter what anyone says. No one should be put in a box.

There's no box big enough to contain all the wonderful things you are!

Avoid "box" conversations! Try answering some of Malibu and Brooklyn's favorite questions:

What's the best thing that happened this week?

_____

What was the last good book you read?

_____

Write your own questions:

_____

_____

_____

_____

I love getting to know you!

Flip the Script

Help your Dream Team turn doubt speak into growth speak! If we focus on our small successes and make room for improvement, any dream can be met. Circle the phrase that will help our friends to grow, rather than shrink.

A. Let me try it again.
B. I can't do it.

A. This is as good as it's going to get.
B. I did my best, look at that!

A. I talk too much and too fast.
B. I have many important things to say!

A. I made it past the finish line and had fun doing it.
B. I tried so hard and still came in second place.

A. If I stop now, I will never finish.
B. If I take a break now, I will feel better when finishing up later.

Answers: A, B, B, A, B

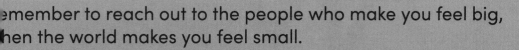

Remember to reach out to the people who make you feel big, when the world makes you feel small.

Circle some ways you can always keep those people close.

Write them a letter.

Send them a text message or email.

Hang up their photo in your room.

Call them for their birthday.

Write your own ideas:

_____

I called home a lot when I went to summer camp. I was only a few miles from my family, but I wanted to feel closer to them. They give me strength!

I AM ENOUGH!

My name is

_____

and I am smart enough, strong enough,
and good enough to be anything.